'Haiku's of the Heart.'

of the

SHANNON GOWENS

To order additional copies of this book, contact:
Xlibris
844-714-8691
www.Xlibris.com
Orders@Xlibris.com

ISBN: Softcover   978-1-6698-2447-3
         EBook   978-1-6698-2448-0

Print information available on the last page

Rev. date: 05/06/2022

Control

I want to show strength
I want to say more with less
Gain the upper hand

They Melt my Heart

Made from my body
I bore them and know them well
The thought gives me joy

Sunshine

She is the flower
Opening to the sunlight
Bloom - she makes me smile

Drama

Ugh - I don't want it
Ever - keep it to yourselves
Own it or let it go

Compassion

They talk and touch – kind
They say thanks for their being
Dark waters run deep

Racism

When I watch the news
I slump - hands to face - cry soft
That could be my son

Heartbreak

When I saw you hug
When she leaned on your shoulder
The heavy weight I felt

Text

I wrote you last night
I had so much bottled up
Your soul can't hear me

Insecure

I'm afraid of you
Afraid of judgement - group thoughts
I don't deserve shame

Wake up Call

Soft repetition
A hum of a bell - constant ring
Pavlov - we respond

Evil Eye Necklace

I gave it to him
And he tangled the gold chain
I fixed it quietly

My Son

Are you ready son?
Face responsibility
Love without question

I Say too Much

I desire praise
Or at least comfort - a look
So I can relax

Headache

I seek distraction
Something to shift my focus
Away from the drum

Youth

She has potential
I see her strength - what I was
Be smarter than me

Magnets

I spoke of this once
Truly felt I understood
Doubt I ever will

Uncomfortable

I'm working on it
The itch - the hunt - I contain
I breathe and fidget

Fear

The time is so close
We can't avoid forever
I'm afraid of it

Maturity

I spoke with her once
Not really - just text message
I wish we had more time

Color

Our love was light pink
Then it thickened to dark red
Now it bleeds sky blue

Disappointment

The fear of your hate
Shadowed by your disinterest
Why's that so much worse?

Shallow

It was always light
Your look - lust - mattress, then door
You found love - strange – sad

Eggshells

My breath is help tight
My foot is delicate step
I am not myself

Deep

I mourn out memories
Your photos give me comfort
I consult your eyes

I'm Not the One

To babysit this
These friends that can't hold their own
I'm not your mother

Humanity

What does that mean here?
What do you - do we stand for?
Ask your soul - respond

Printed in the United States
by Baker & Taylor Publisher Services